I want to give a special thanks to:

Cindy, for being my sounding board, encourager, and rock

Danielle as my chief editor

My family who encourage me to pursue dreams

All the Dgroup members that have helped my spiritual journey

Robby Gallaty and Tim LaFleur for providing a blueprint for discipleship

All those who bought Blackberry Wisdom and encouraged me

YOU for giving this book a try

Jesus for being everything to me

Preface

As a follow-up to my first book *Blackberry Wisdom*, I wanted to write a Bible study using the scriptures referenced in that book. I took time to select the scriptures used in that book because of their relevance to me and my stories, but I didn't take the time to explore the scriptures fully. In this book, I want to explore the truths of these scriptures and how they apply to our lives.

The other reason I wrote this book was to share with you what I have found to be a fantastic guide for forming a daily habit of personal quiet time.

I know that praying and reading my Bible daily is essential for my well-being and maturity in Christ. I also found that if I write down what I think God is saying to me each day, it solidifies what I am hearing, and over a period of time those words become encouraging and helpful in developing my faith.

I hope this book serves as a model for you to spend daily time reading God's word and communicating with Him. I call this "quiet time." You may have another name for your time with the Lord, but the general idea is to spend time with God reading His Word and quietly listening to His voice.

I have heard that we retain about 15% of what we read and 75% of what we practice or write. So writing what we are reading and hearing gives us a much better chance of remembering and actually living it out in our lives.

When I was younger, I enjoyed white water rafting. In the nearby Ocoee River, navigating downstream was unsafe unless you had some experience on that particular river. One way you gained experience was by going down the river several times with a guide.

A river guide knows the best route and the places to avoid. They also know how to guide you to places where you get the maximum adrenaline rush!

The picture below shows me on one of those trips. Our river guide is in the back, focused on looking ahead and barking out row commands. The passionate individual in front of him is me just having a blast that day.

On this trip, I was not thinking about navigating down the river again by myself, so paying close attention to our course was really not something I had on my mind that day. I was just there for the adrenaline rush!

Had I decided to come back one day and go down the river by myself, I think I would have paid a lot closer attention to my guide and why he did what he did.

I hope you will do just that - pay attention to this guide. See how the prayers offered put you in the proper posture to hear from God. Read His word, understand His word, and then let His word guide and direct your daily life!

Write in this book. Take notes on what you hear, learn, and feel. Mark it up with colored pens or pencils. Hey, you bought the book – use it to maximize your efforts!

I have heard that if we commit to something for 21 straight days it will become a habit.

I think if you follow the daily pattern laid out in this book, you will find a routine that can help develop your relationship with Jesus. If you follow this routine for the 21 days I've laid out, it will help you develop proper habits.

I believe you will find that you hear from the Lord better, and the new adventures He guides you to will only increase your faith!

I want this book to serve you. Serve as a guide for your quiet time with Jesus that turns into life-breathing habits! So stick to it for 21 days if you can. Let this book help form life-breathing habits in your life.

As a disciple of Jesus, this should be a daily routine we follow to deepen and develop our relationship with God. Don't read and pray out of obligation but out of a desire to hear from our Creator. Yes – we are communicating with the God who created US! There is no better use of our time in a day than spending it growing closer to the God who knows us intimately and sustains us daily.

Our goal should be to make more time for God in our schedule through quiet time and constant prayer. Our quiet time should be carved out and intentionally set aside every day. When we do that, we can get to a place where we find ourselves talking to God all day long. Spending time with God is the most rewarding, satisfying, and day-guiding activity we can do. The more – the better!

Suggested Quiet Time schedule

This suggested quiet time should take somewhere between five to fifteen minutes each day. You can rush it, or you can spend more time with God. If you have spent any time with God you know more is better.

Pray – Confess your sins to God and ask Him to forgive you. Recognize how great He is. Ask Him to open your heart and bless your time in His Word. Then pray for others and situations heavy on your heart.

Read Scripture Read from your favorite translation or the included text. The scriptures quoted in this book are from the Holman Christian Standard Bible (HSCB) translation.

Read the provided explanation and application

Read the daily Scripture again

Tell God your thoughts, desires, struggles, thanksgivings, and supplications.

Meditate quietly, listening for God. Don't talk – listen.

Journal your thoughts and what God shares with you.

Act on the daily direction God provides.

I hope you see that the provided prayers are prayers that you can replicate every day. There is a pattern to the written prayers. Obviously, the written prayers here are just a guide for you, but they contain the proper attitude of what I believe to be the starting point of a good prayer life with God.

When studying Scripture, I use the H.E.A.R. method that I learned in discipleship training from Robby Gallaty and Tim LeFleur. I know there are other great models, so feel free to use the one that helps you get God's Word into you.

To be honest, the best model for studying and applying God's word to your life - is the model that you will use daily.

The **H.E.A.R.** method is simply a model to write into words what you read and learn about a Scripture passage. The method will also help you understand what you need to do as a result of hearing from God through His word.

Highlight

What verses from the Scripture that I am reading stand out to me? Write the actual text of the scripture, including book, chapter, and verse(s).

Explain

What is the context? Who is speaking to whom? What is happening? Where are they located and what is their purpose?

Apply

How can I apply this Biblical truth to my life? The author had an intent for their reader, but those same principal truths can apply directly to me.

Response

What do I need to do in response to the Scripture?
Do I need to take some action or offer a prayer to Jesus?

In this book I have completed the **H E A** and some of the **R** as a guide.

You can download a clean copy of this model for yourself at:
blackberrywisdom.com/hear

Day 1

Wisdom

Prayer: God, please forgive me of the things I have done against You, and for the things I should have done for You but didn't. Please speak directly to my heart as I read Your Word. Thank you for the wisdom You give me and help me to use it wisely. Please bless our time together. In the precious name of Jesus I pray, amen.

The fear of the Lord is the beginning of wisdom, and the knowledge of the Holy One is understanding. For by Wisdom your days will be many, and years will be added to your life.
Proverbs 9:10–11

Explanation

Solomon writes that fear of God is the beginning of wisdom. He is conveying this thought that there is a start to being wise, or a starting point. That starting point is the fear of God. But the fear here is not properly translated as scared but by being in awe and giving reverence. Once you understand how big, powerful, and holy God is, then you are on the path of being wise. You are at the starting point of revering God.

You can look up different definitions of the word wisdom, but let me share my simple definition.

Wisdom is having knowledge and knowing what to do with it.

Would you agree with that definition?

With that definition of wisdom, we see then that once we realize there is a God who created all that we know with just His breath, then our response is to be in awe or to give reverence to God. He is more wonderful than our minds could ever comprehend! Once you begin to understand the wonder of God, how could you not be in total awe?

Application

When I think of giving reverence to God, I think of His holiness and how I am not holy. I humbly realize that I am a mere man. As humans, we will never be perfect like God. I can only draw closer to Him and reflect on His greatness.

But we do have access to knowing more about God through His Word and prayer. The question then becomes, what do I do with the current knowledge I have of God?

Remember wisdom is having knowledge and knowing what to do with it. If I want to know more about God, I will love Him more and then want to share that love! How exactly do we do that?

First, I think we should **want** to know more about Him. Why would you not want to know more about the God who created you, who knows everything about you, and who has everything in His control?

Secondly, knowing more about God makes us **love** Him more. Loving Him more will compel us to spend more time with Him and properly give credit for all the wonderful things in our life. By spending more time with God, we grow in wisdom because He will tell us what to do with the knowledge we are gaining. That is how we can grow in wisdom!

Then thirdly, I think we should **share** that relationship with others. Why would we not want to share what we know about God, and how we communicate with Him to our family, friends, and those who we come in contact with on a daily basis?

Response

Thank God today for the wisdom He has given you.

Who needs to be encouraged by hearing about your relationship with God today?

Meditation

Read **Proverbs 9:10–11** in your Bible. Then meditate, pray, and journal what God is saying to you.

What part of this scripture can you recall all during the day?

Day 2

Picking Partners

Prayer: God, please forgive me of the things I have done against You, and for the things I should have done for You but didn't. Please speak directly to my heart as I read Your Word. Thank you for the friends You have put in my life. Please bless our time together. In the precious name of Jesus I pray, amen.

A friend loves at all times,
and a brother is born for a difficult time.
Proverbs 17:17

Explanation

Solomon describes two kinds of partners that will be close to us in our life: a friend and a brother.

True friends love each other with what I believe to be the highest Greek term for love – *philia*.

Philia is a deep, powerful emotional bond between two people. It is a love based on mutual respect and a shared devotion or interest. Some say *philia* love is greater than *agape* love. *Agape* love is an unconditional love, but *philia* is that unconditional love with shared interests.

We are told to love everyone – those we like and those we don't like. When we love people we like and share common interests, that gives us more reasons to want to love them.

Application

How do we love those that we consider friends? Some of those are easy, but some require a little more work. To be honest, we are not always easy to love.

As our seasons of life change, we grow further away from some friends and closer to others. That is really a part of the maturing process of adults. Our life situations and interests change. The same could be said about our friends. We all change with the seasons of life.

With those changes, we sometimes neglect to show love toward our friends. How? By not doing things for them. By not doing as many activities with them. And sometimes it's as simple as not communicating with them the way we should.

Do your friends know you love them? How do they know? Because of your actions or because of your words? Love is a feeling when it pleases you, and love is an action when it pleases others.

Response

Sometimes it is good to just evaluate the way we show love to our friends. They want our love – just like you want theirs.

What friend(s) do you need to call or visit today?

_____

_____

_____

Meditation

Read **Proverbs 9:10–11** in your Bible. Then meditate and journal what God is saying to you.

What part of this scripture can you recall all during the day?

Day 3

Family Harmony

Prayer: God, please forgive me of the things I have done against You, and for the things I should have done for You but didn't. Please speak directly to my heart as I read Your Word. Thank you for my family. Please bless our time together.
In the precious name of Jesus I pray,
amen.

How good and pleasant it is
when brothers live together in harmony!
Psalm 133:1

Explanation

The Bible records that King David had at least twenty sons by seven different wives.

So, when David says it is good and pleasant when brothers live in harmony, I believe he has a pretty good understanding of what harmony looks like and doesn't look like. I would venture a guess that he saw both ends of the spectrum (peace and quarrels) and was remembering just how wonderful it is when all the family is in harmony.

His description was "how good and pleasant it is." I believe the "good" part is in relationship with others. It was good with the other brothers when all the family got along. Meaning they had peace with each other.

By "pleasant" David was referencing from his point of view. Oh, how it pleased David to see his family living in harmony. How pleasant it is for any father to see his family in harmony.

Harmony, in short, means to be in agreement. In musical terms, it means to blend a combination of tones into a sound that is pleasing to the ear. It also means to have a pleasing arrangement of parts. For David, I am sure that harmony meant when all his family was in agreement with each other in such a way that it was pleasing to the ear.

Application

Just like David could see and understand when his family was in agreement, I believe we can see the same within our own families.

We can understand and appreciate when there is harmony in our family and experience frustration when there is not.

Can every family be in complete agreement? I don't think so. As humans, we have such a variety of experiences and biases that make it hard for two people to agree often, and the more people you add to the mix, the less likely that a common agreement can be found.

Sometimes we should just agree that it is ok to disagree.

Does God make perfect families? Again, I don't think so. I think God makes families that fit into His perfect plan.

But where are the places that we can agree? As a believer in Jesus, we should all be able to find common ground at the foot of the cross. We should all be able to agree on the foundational commands that Jesus gave his disciples, which also apply to us in today's world.

Love God and love others. These are foundational truths that should guide how we live our daily lives. We should all find those two commands as a starting point.

Now how do we love God and, in turn, love others? I would say we would disagree on this to some degree. Even in how we love God we can agree there are different ways to do so, but at the end of the day, we should be able to trace the root of the desire back to the fact that we love God. In that fact we can be in harmony!

Response

Is there a family member that you need to find common ground with in order to live in harmony?

Is there a family member you need to forgive or ask for forgiveness and then agree to love God and love others together?

Meditation

Read **Psalm 133:1** in your Bible. Then meditate and journal what God is saying to you.

What part of this scripture can you recall all during the day?

Day 4

Love

Prayer: God, please forgive me of the things I have done against You, and for the things I should have done for You but didn't. Please speak directly to my heart as I read Your Word. Thank you for the example of how to love. Please bless our time together.
In the precious name of Jesus I pray,
amen.

*If I speak human or angelic languages
but do not have love,
I am a sounding gong or a clanging cymbal.
If I have the gift of prophecy
and understand all mysteries and all knowledge,
and if I have all faith so that I can move mountains
but do not have love, I am nothing.
And if I donate all my goods to feed the poor,
and if I give my body in order to boast
but do not have love, I gain nothing.
Love is patient, love is kind.
Love does not envy, is not boastful, is not conceited,
does not act improperly, is not selfish, is not provoked,
and does not keep a record of wrongs.
Love finds no joy in unrighteousness but rejoices in the truth.
It bears all things, believes all things,
hopes all things, endures all things.
Love never ends.*
1 Corinthians 13:1-8

Explanation

Paul reminds the Corinthians not to be over zealous of their spiritual gifts, like the gift of tongues or languages. He says they are meaningless without love.

He also said the gift of prophecy, knowledge, and faith to do miracles has no value apart from love.

If you give all your possessions, even right down to your very body, with the expectation of personal gain then it is for nothing. You must do it out of love.

The love that Paul is describing is the *agape* love. Love that is unconditional. Love that doesn't care if we are loved back.

Then Paul starts to describe love.

Love is patient	Love is kind
Love does not envy	Love is not boastful
Love is not conceited	Love does not act improperly
Love is not selfish	Love is not provoked
Love does not keep a record of wrongs	Love rejoices in truth
Love finds no joy in unrighteousness	Love believes all things
Love bears all things	Love endures all things
Love hopes all things	

Love never ends

The love we are talking about here is an action – not a feeling.

Application

At this point, you might ask yourself – how do I know if I am a loving person? First, you could just ask others, and if they were honest, they might tell you ways in which you do and do not show love.

Another way is to discern for yourself by inserting your name for the word love. Write your name in each blank below and listen as God confirms whether you are loving in this way.

_____ is patient   _____ is not conceited

_____ is kind   _____ does not act

_____ does not envy   improperly

_____ is not boastful

_____ is not selfish   _____ rejoices in truth

_____ is not provoked   _____ bears all things

_____ does not keep a   _____ believes all things

record of wrongs   _____ hopes all things

_____ finds no joy in   _____ endures all things

unrighteousness

_____'s love never ends

Response

Read over the list again with your name inserted. Circle the love descriptions you feel you need to work on.

Maybe you need to ask others if you are loving in these ways.

You might want to pray and ask God to show you where you need to focus some efforts to become a more loving person.

Meditation

Read **1 Corinthians 13** in your bible. Then meditate and journal what God is saying to you.

What part of this scripture can you recall all during the day?

Day 5

Encourage

Prayer: God, please forgive me of the things I have done against You, and for the things I should have done for You but didn't. Please speak directly to my heart as I read Your Word. Thank you for how You encourage me! Please bless our time together. In the precious name of Jesus I pray, amen.

Therefore encourage one another and build each other up as you are already doing.
1 Thessalonians 5:11

Explanation

Paul shares that the early Christians know Jesus will return like a thief in the night – unexpectantly. We, as Christians, are children of the day. Meaning that we are not saved to participate in anything that satan prepares in the dark and that we should not be surprised when Jesus comes back. We are to always be ready and watching for His return.

The word "ready" means we are to be spiritually and morally alert. We are watching out for temptation and exercising self-control during these hard times on earth.

We are to be self-controlled by putting on the armor of God so that we can stand against the tactics of the devil. Our battle is not against flesh and blood, but the dark spiritual forces of this world. See the whole armor of God in Ephesians 6:10-18.

Here in 1 Thessalonians 5, Paul tells us to encourage one another. As Christians, it is our responsibility to encourage others as they try to deny temptations and be self-controlled.

Paul says if you are already encouraging, then do even more! Encourage more often or encourage more people.

Application

Encouragement – the action of giving support, confidence, or hope.

I think of my D-group when I think of encouragement. A D-group (discipleship group) is a small group (4-6 members) of the same gender who meet weekly for a year to study God's Word and become more like Jesus.

In the D-groups I have participated in over the years, we have learned to know each other through our spiritual discussions and doing life together. It is from this group of men that I seek encouragement and accountability. They are my go-to group!

In addition to my D-group, my wife is my first encourager. My wife knows my history and who I really am. I also have other family members and friends who have the ability to encourage me.

How do we encourage others? Based on the definition, we encourage with an action. That action can be a word of praise, or a word to build confidence during a trial. Encourage someone to stay engaged until the end or that there are better days ahead. It could also be a word of hope. We could also encourage by an action of joining someone in the effort in which they are engaged. Just come alongside and help.

As disciples of Jesus, we need to know that there are others in the battle with us. We need to know that they have struggles just like we do. And then we need to encourage them to continue the good fight of denying worldly sin and to follow Jesus daily!

This world is only becoming more sinful, and disciples need encouragement to keep their focus on Jesus always.

Response

Who are your go-to people and groups for encouragement?

Who comes to you for encouragement?

Who around you today needs encouragement? There is certainly somebody. Seek to encourage as many people as possible today! Find something they are doing correctly and bring that to their attention.

Meditation

Read **1 Thessalonians 5:1-11** in your Bible. Then meditate and journal what God is saying to you.

What part of this scripture can you recall all during the day?

Day 6

Bad Company

Prayer: God, please forgive me of the things I have done against You, and for the things I should have done for You but didn't. Please speak directly to my heart as I read Your Word. Thank you for how You encourage me when no one is looking! Please bless our time together. In the precious name of Jesus I pray, amen.

Do not be deceived: "Bad company corrupts good morals."
1 Corinthians 15:33

Explanation

Paul is telling the church in Corinth to come to their senses and stop sinning. Specifically, he is affirming the resurrection of Jesus and rebuking those who would believe and teach differently. He tells them not to be ignorant about Jesus but to listen to what he has preached and taught.

He tells them not to be deceived by those who are considered bad company because they will lead them astray from the truth. They would cause them to follow a false teaching rather than the truth.

The false teachers would corrupt good morals that they understood to be true. Another way to interpret the good morals is to say that it was the communion the church had with each other. But more importantly, they were corrupting the church by leading them from the foundational truths of Jesus to a worldly view of Jesus.

Application

Morals are defined as the right or wrong human action and character. It also means to conform to the standards of what is right or proper behavior.

If we can agree on this definition, then the next question is who determines what is right or proper behavior? For us Christians, God sets our standards. For non-Christians, who knows what or who sets their standards.

I believe that as disciples of Jesus we should be careful to know who we are listening to and why.

Does our pastor preach God's Word correctly? How do you know? Do you get your Bible out and read as He reads while preaching? If he is not reading from the Bible or rightfully dissecting God's Word then I believe you should discuss it with him. Not in a scornful way, but in a way that you both might understand and be drawn closer to God.

Does your Sunday School teacher do the same? Do you follow along in your Bible and take notes? In those smaller settings, you have more liberty to speak up. I am not suggesting challenging a leader in a group setting, but ask questions. Questions are how we all learn.

Are your friends influencing you in the right direction? If they are leading you away from Jesus, then maybe you should distance yourself from them and associate with friends who help draw you closer to Jesus.

What about your music, entertainment, and hobbies – do they help draw you closer or further away from Jesus?

I thought of a little diagram that helps me decide if I am drawing myself and others closer or further away from Jesus with the following.

Place the following words in the cloud and think: *Is that drawing me closer to or away from Jesus?*

Jesus

MY ACTIONS
MY THOUGHTS
MY FRIENDS
FAMILY
JOB
SERVICE
MUSIC
ENTERTAINMENT

Response

It is good to take an evaluation of the influences in your life that draw you closer to Jesus and those that pull you away. In that inventory, you might want to clean out some bad company or habits to be sure your morals are not compromised.

Take time to consider your:
- Daily Actions
- Thoughts
- Friends
- Family
- Job
- Service to others
- Music
- Entertainment
- Hobbies

Are each of these drawing you closer to or further away from Jesus?

If further away, what needs to change?

Meditation

Read **1 Corinthians 15:33-34** in your Bible. Then meditate and journal what God is saying to you.

What part of this scripture can you recall all during the day?

Day 7

Sweet Rewards

Prayer: God, please forgive me of the things I have done against You, and for the things I should have done for You but didn't. Please speak directly to my heart as I read Your Word. Thank you for how You continually bless me! Please bless our time together. In the precious name of Jesus I pray, amen.

Honor the Lord with your possessions and with the first produce of your entire harvest; then your barns will be completely filled, and your vats will overflow with new wine.
Proverbs 3:9-10

Explanation

Honoring the Lord with our possessions is another way of saying *trust the Lord with all your heart,* as proclaimed in Proverbs 3:5. Honor here is associated with sacrifice. We could say this similarly by saying honor God by sacrificing our best to Him. Our possessions are basically all that we have and have acquired.

Then Solomon also says honor God with our first fruits. This principle of giving the first fruits means the best fruits, which are the finest and the healthiest. The first fruits are highly anticipated by the grower, and the next fruits are not always guaranteed. He is saying to give our very best to God, and then God will honor them by providing even more.

It would seem that this is a hidden Biblical equation:

First possessions + First fruits = Filled barns and vats

But in reality, this is the focus of a relationship with God, not an equation.

Solomon says that when we honor God with our best, God will honor us with His best. Really, he is saying you can't outgive God! God will richly reward those who honor Him with their best.

To the Hebrews, a filled barn would mean less worry and more contentment. It means they have properly prepared the family or flock to be sustainable.

Vats overflowing meant plentifulness and without want. The new wine would be strong, flavorful, and wonderful.

A more proper alignment than the above equation would be:

Our Best + God = Content

Application

When I think of giving to God, I have to be honest, at times I think I need to be sure that I am taking care of myself and my family instead of giving it to God and allowing Him to provide the abundance. And I know He will! Why do I doubt Him?!

From my money, job, talents, family, and time I need to focus on giving it to God and allow Him to bless me.

I believe when we get that in order, He will bless us in ways that we cannot even imagine.

James 1:17 says, "Every generous act and every perfect gift is from above, coming down from the Father of lights."

Now don't misunderstand me. I am not promoting a prosperity gospel at all. There will be tough times in life, no doubt. The wonder of it all is when I focus on giving to God, He blesses me in a way that just blows my mind! When God blesses, it truly is a blessing! Like a blackberry pie in July, God's blessings are such a sweet reward in this life!

Response

What parts of your life are you honoring to God and which parts do you honor yourself?

Of all you have and all you are – what is the best? Do you give that best to God?

Meditation

Read **Proverbs 3:9-10** in your Bible. Then meditate and journal what God is saying to you.

What part of this scripture can you recall all during the day?

Day 8

Tranquil Thoughts

Prayer: God, please forgive me of the things I have done against You, and for the things I should have done for You but didn't. Please speak directly to my heart as I read Your Word. Thank you for Your peace! Please bless our time together.
In the precious name of Jesus I pray,
amen.

A patient person shows great understanding, but a quick-tempered one promotes foolishness. A tranquil heart is life to the body, but jealousy is rottenness to the bones.
Proverbs 14:29-30

Explanation

Patience is the ability to wait calmly when confronted with a delay or suffering. On the other hand, a quick-tempered person is easily made angry.

Why is it that a patient person shows great understanding? Maybe it is because the patient person is exercising wisdom in a situation. They know to control their response after a situation has played out instead of jumping to a quick conclusion. Wisdom can help a person exercise patience.

Solomon says that a tranquil heart is life to the body. Life brings about health, goodness, fruitfulness, and abundance. A tranquil heart is healthy for the body. The tranquil heart is rested and ready to determine the correct course of action.

By contrast, an agitated heart would bring stagnation which leads to being rotten. Solomon says not only a rotten part of the body, but rotten all the way to the bones. A fruit that is rotten is only good to be thrown out and will soon return to dust.

In Hebrew, this word *jealous* describes an intense fervor, passion, and emotion that is greater than a person's anger. Some Bible translations use the words envy, jealousy, or passion for this term.

Jealousy can be used in either a good or bad way, but here Solomon indicates he is showing us what happens when passion is focused in a bad way. Being jealous for God is good, but being jealous for our own passions is bad.

Application

One way to practice calmness is to first know how to find it or get back to it. We need to have a starting point of calmness or a place where we can return to calm. The easiest way for me to get calm is to talk to Jesus. He is my source of patience and calmness. I need to have a time each day where I find peace and get in touch with that calming voice.

At a minimum, I need a few minutes a day to pray to God. Praying completely – sharing my burdens with Him and listening to what He has to say to me. Alone time with Jesus is my set point for the day, and all good thoughts and direction come from what He shares with me.

Then when something is delayed or goes bad in my day, I can easily remember back to when I was talking to my God who created me. When someone does something that angers me in the day, I reflect on that time that Jesus calmed me through our earlier conversation.

Having a daily place of rest in Jesus helps me when I need it the most.

Response

When is your daily time with Jesus? Your quiet time?

Do you need to adjust something in your life to allow time to sit and share your burdens with God and listen to the direction He has for you each day?

Meditation

Read **Proverbs 14:29-30** in your Bible. Then meditate and journal what God is saying to you.

What time and how long does God want to spend with you each day?

Day 9

Love Each Other Deeply

Prayer: God, please forgive me of the things I have done against You, and for the things I should have done for You but didn't. Please speak directly to my heart as I read Your Word. Thank you for how You love me! Please bless our time together.
In the precious name of Jesus I pray,
amen.

Above all, maintain an intense love for each other, since love covers a multitude of sins. Be hospitable to one another without complaining. Based on the gift each one has received, use it to serve others, as good managers of the varied grace of God.
1 Peter 4:8-10

Explanation

"An intense love for each other." Other translations use constant love, fervent love, or love deeply. The idea here is to love just as much as you possibly can. Peter is telling those that have a common relationship with Jesus to love each other to the best of their ability.

That kind of love, Peter says, covers a multitude of sins - sins of the person who is loving and the person who is the object of that love. It is through this kind of Christian fellowship that small things that offend can be easily cleared up. Putting a lot of love in a relationship makes those trivial differences small or nonexistent.

Remember the love discussed here is an action, not a feeling.

One way to show love is others is to be hospitable toward them. To open a home and share the blessings both have received by the grace of God is a way to be hospitable. Peter says to do this without grumbling that one person is giving more than the other.

Then he tells them to use the gift that God has given to each believer. Those gifts are varied from believer to believer and would include but are not limited to:

- Administration
- Evangelism
- Faith
- Healing
- Hospitality
- Leadership
- Prophecy
- Teaching

- Discernment
- Exhortation
- Giving
- Helps
- Knowledge
- Mercy
- Serving
- Wisdom

Application

We use our spiritual gifts to serve the people in the church. For most, that is the church in which we are a member. You can't serve the church by watching a preacher on TV. You must be an active part of a church body to use your gifts accordingly.

I love to serve in my church because by doing so I know that I am exercising the gifts God has given me like teaching, serving, and giving. I believe there is no greater joy on earth than to be operating the way God designed me and serving the people who love Him the way I do.

I also enjoy helping other churches that have a need. This doesn't happen often, but when brothers and sisters in Christ need help with resources that I have available, then I am more than happy to share!

Response

How are you loving the people in your church? Now that you are learning more about God and listening to His voice, is there a better way that you should love and serve them?

Maybe you need to love some people more deeply or maybe you need to love more people.

Meditation

Read **1 Peter 4:7-11** in your Bible. Then meditate and journal what God is saying to you.

Is God asking you to love more deeply or to love more people?

What part of this scripture can you recall all during the day?

Day 10

Life is Difficult

Prayer: God, please forgive me of the things I have done against You, and for the things I should have done for You but didn't. Please speak directly to my heart as I read Your Word. Thank you for how You are with me in difficult times! Please bless our time together.
In the precious name of Jesus I pray,
amen.

The fear of the Lord is the beginning of knowledge; fools despise wisdom and discipline.
Proverbs 1:7

Explanation

Solomon explains that the fear of God is the beginning of knowledge. In other words, the beginning point of knowledge is the fear of God. It serves as the foundation for where God will make a person wise in His eyes.

But the fear described here is not properly translated as being scared, but by being in awe and showing proper reverence. It is only appropriate for the created to revere their Creator. Understanding that relationship is the beginning of our knowledge.

The term fool is a contrast used in the Old Testament to differentiate between the faithful and sinners – those who belong to God's family and those who do not. In Hebrew terms, a fool was someone who was considered a waste of time to try to instruct.

Solomon said that the fool doesn't want to adhere to God's wisdom and instruction. The fool doesn't want to follow the Law of God or humbly participate in His family. He was instructing listeners to hear and adhere to the wisdom of the Proverbs, and not wind up like the fool.

Application

The fact is our life on this earth is difficult. And difficult as it is, it would be worse without the comfort, love, and direction from our Heavenly Father.

I don't know about you, but I really don't like to be corrected. I think that I have all the wisdom I need to function correctly in life. And that is where I make it harder on myself. I need God's correction because it is good for me.

We tell our children to stay away from a hot stove. Why? Because we don't want them to get hurt. It is not a privilege or treat we are taking away; it is to keep them from harm. We, as parents, know better than a child. In the same way, God, as our Creator, knows what is best for us if we will listen to His voice.

I believe that God has wisdom for me during difficult times. That is where I believe this proverb comes into play. If we will listen to the knowledge and abide by that knowledge we will grow in wisdom. We don't want to be like the fool and grow away from God – but rather closer to Him!

I think you would agree - life is difficult. We need to stay close to the Master and follow His instruction to help lessen some of the difficulty. Jesus said in Matthew 11:30, "My yoke is easy and My burden is light."

Response

What difficult times are you experiencing right now?

What situations in your life are you listening to God? What situations in your life are you listening to yourself or to the world?

Meditation

Read **Proverbs 1:7** in your Bible. Then meditate and journal what God is saying to you.

What part of this scripture can you recall all during the day?

Day 11

Honor One Another

Prayer: God, please forgive me of the things I have done against You, and for the things I should have done for You but didn't. Please speak directly to my heart as I read Your Word. Thank you for how You show me how to be humble. Please bless our time together. In the precious name of Jesus I pray, amen.

Love must be without hypocrisy. Detest evil; cling to what is good. Show family affection to one another with brotherly love. Outdo one another in showing honor.
Romans 12:9-10

Explanation

Hypocrisy is doing something you tell someone else not to do or engaging in behavior that contradicts your professed feelings or beliefs. In other words, love with hypocrisy is not really love at all, but rather a charade in which someone pretends to love when they do not.

Paul says to detest the evil in this world – stay away from it. He warns us not to give evil any chance to take hold in our lives, but to allow only the goodness of God to be a part of who we are. We should hold tightly to the things that God has shown to be good in this world.

The brotherly love mentioned here is the type of love that Christians should have for one another by considering others in the faith our brother or sister in Christ. If the church can treat others this way, then that church is demonstrating the hallmark of love outlined in this chapter. Paul was showing them a better way to act in love as a church.

Then he gives this metaphor of winning against another - do it to show the most honor. The Greeks put a great emphasis on games like the

Olympics in their culture. They would certainly appreciate the challenge of outdoing someone. If they had this desire for competition in them, then Paul says to see who can show the most honor to another.

To the church in Rome, Paul is saying to love and honor one another with the goodness they know from God.

Application

Today, honor is not a word used very often. I hear it sometimes in honoring our military personnel, Veterans, or first responders, but rarely do I see the term used much. Do you?

Just what does it mean to honor someone, and how do you do it?

To me, honoring someone is to put their wants and needs ahead of mine - to show respect toward another with the idea that they are more important to me. It is rooted in being humble, and in our world today, humbleness is not valued or applauded.

Jesus demonstrated the ultimate humility through His example on earth. He said in Matthew 20:28 that He came to this world not to be served but to serve. We should learn to be humble and serve others just like Jesus.

I believe this is the way we love those we do not like – or our enemies. We must humble ourselves before them and love them like Jesus commanded.

Philippians 2:3 says in humility count others more significant than yourselves. We have to be in that mindset to those that we really do not like - deserve our love, and that can only come from a humble posture.

Response

Evaluate the people you honor in your life and those whom you would never consider in that category. What is the difference? Is it your ability to become humble?

Talk to God about your heart first and realize that anything good you can do must come from God.

Humble yourself.

Then consider those whom who you need to love by honoring them first.

Now ... what would Jesus have you do next?

Meditation

Read **Romans 12:9-10** in your Bible. Then meditate and journal what God is saying to you.

What part of this scripture can you recall all during the day?

Day 12

Pain is Certain

Prayer: God, please forgive me of the things I have done against You, and for the things I should have done for You but didn't. Please speak directly to my heart as I read Your Word. Thank you for how You correctly discipline me. Please bless our time together.
In the precious name of Jesus I pray,
amen.

Do not despise the Lord's instruction, my son, and do not loathe His discipline; for the Lord disciplines the one He loves, just as a father, the son he delights in.
Proverbs 3:11-12

Explanation

Solomon is giving sound advice to his son here. He breaks it into two parts: a father's instruction and his discipline.

The instruction of a father is the way he should live. Solomon knows a father has more wisdom than a son simply because he has lived more years – he has seen more heartache and tries to steer a son away from trouble. A good father will explain the direction and the potential problems and expect a good son to follow that direction.

When that son does not follow the direction given, a good father will then discipline. From a very early age until a child comes of age, a parent has to discipline them. It is commanded in the Bible, and it is absolutely what is best for the child.

Solomon gives the analogy that the Lord disciplines all His children in love, just like a father or mother disciplines their children in love. Discipline should not come out of anger, but of love. Parents discipline their children because they love them.

Application

At a certain age we figure out that our disciplining has come to an end. We think that at a certain age mom and dad have raised me the best they can, and now I will not be disciplined anymore. But that is just not true – my mom and dad still discipline me today.

God has been and will continue to discipline us until we are made perfect in His sight. Even our parents can discipline us as adults when needed – we are still their children.

God will bring to our attention or allow some discomfort in our life to correct the sin we have in our life. It may not be immediate, but God will discipline us to conform us to His plan for us.

He wants us to correct sin in our lives. Sin that is both seen and unseen, willful sin, and sins of ignorance. We are so full of sin that we need discipline from God every day.

God wants to draw us closer to Him. Any move contrary to that, He will allow us to be disciplined to be trained to do the right thing. And for us humans, sometimes that is just painful.

Because of Genesis 3 we live in a fallen world, and there will always be pain for us. We should find pleasure in being trained and becoming more like Jesus – that is our ultimate goal in life. Correct discipline is when we allow that pain to correct our sinful ways and be drawn to Jesus.

Response

In what ways is God disciplining you? In what ways is He providing a training ground that will make you more like Jesus?

Ask God to show you in your struggles how He wants you to be more like Him.

Meditation

Read **Proverbs 3:11-12** in your Bible. Then meditate and journal what God is saying to you.

What part of this scripture can you recall all during the day?

Day 13

Hard Work

Prayer: God, please forgive me of the things I have done against You, and for the things I should have done for You but didn't. Please speak directly to my heart as I read Your Word. Thank you for how You have made me for hard work. Please bless our time together.
In the precious name of Jesus I pray,
amen.

Go to the ant, you slacker! Observe its ways and become wise. Without leader, administrator, or ruler, it prepares its provisions in summer; it gathers its food during harvest. How long will you stay in bed, you slacker? When will you get up from your sleep?
Proverbs 6:6-9

Explanation

I just love the way Solomon calls out the lazy person here! He is not cutting them any slack. He tells this human to learn how to work from a lowly ant.

Is the slacker one person in particular or a general observation to all who are slackers – people not pulling their weight? We don't know for sure, but I assume this applies to all slackers.

He says the ant does not depend on a manager or boss to tell them what to do. They just naturally get up each day and go about a full day of hard work, with no regard for payment or praise. They simply work hard, and keep on working.

In Proverbs 30:24-25 we see that the ant prepares for the winter by collecting during the summer. They understand the seasons and what work needs to be done at that time to prepare for times when the season isn't as fruitful.

Solomon said to observe or to consider the way an ant works. Then apply that lesson of hard work to their life. Remember wisdom is having correct knowledge and knowing what to do with it.

Then he asks that lazy person how long they plan to stay in bed. Staying in bed or resting for a certain amount of time is good and required by the body, but too much rest makes one lazy.

Application

I learned from an early age to get out of bed and do my chores. My father detested us laying in bed late into the morning when we were in high school. When I was that age I was not full of wisdom. Now, as an adult, I see that staying in bed late in the mornings was just 'burning daylight.' I also learned from picking blackberries to get out into the field early in the morning before it got too hot. Picking was much easier in the cooler part of the day.

God actually created us for work (Gen 1:26-28), and initially, work was good in the garden of Eden. Then after sin entered the world, work became difficult (Gen 3:17-19). Since we are sinful creatures, our work will be hard, and some people try to find a way to keep from work so they can take it easy.

We are also told that our good works are the result of our salvation. If we have accepted the saving grace of Jesus, then we will work to produce fruit in our lives. We don't work for our salvation, but rather as a loving response to salvation, do we work for the Lord.

A good disciple of Jesus will want to work for the Lord!

What is the ultimate work in our lives? To love God and love others. We are obedient to Jesus by making disciples that follow His commands. You can't stay in bed all day and work for the glory of God.

Our love for Jesus is measured in how we love others. Loving others is the only evidential proof that, as disciples, we indeed love Jesus.

Response

How is your current work ethic? How are your works glorifying God? What habits or hobbies do you need to lessen or increase so you can work harder for the glory of God?

Meditation

Read **Proverbs 6:6-9** in your Bible. Then meditate and journal what God is saying to you.

What part of this scripture can you recall all during the day? Are you working hard to try and memorize scripture?

Today is Unpredictable

Prayer: God, please forgive me of the things I have done against You, and for the things I should have done for You but didn't. Please speak directly to my heart as I read Your Word. Thank you for how You have a plan for my life. Please bless our time together.
In the precious name of Jesus I pray,
amen.

A man's heart plans his way, but the Lord determines his steps.
Proverbs 16:9

Explanation

Solomon says it is through the heart that we make our own plans, but only God knows the correct direction we should take. It is through the help of God that a correct action can be taken.

A person's heart is filled with the input he or she receives on a daily basis. From the people we talk to, the music we listen to, the books we read, and the TV we watch – each of these plays a part in adding to the things in our heart and mind.

The heart has input from our eyes, ears, mouth, and hands. That input is processed by the heart and used for output to our mind and decisions.

It is from these inputs we determine what we will do on a given day. We make the plans for the next week or even month with the input from our knowledge and the plans we have in our life.

It is not a bad thing that we plan our ways. God created us with a wonderful mind, and making plans should be a part of our daily routine. I believe that God is a God of order and making plans is right. We should probably spend more time carefully planning our day and week.

But all of our planning should not be determined by only our own minds. We should listen to God and see what He has in store for us each day. We should humbly submit our daily plans to God and determine if that is the direction He has for us.

God knows the outcome of our day before it even starts. He also knows what tomorrow will hold. Our best hope is to rely on the daily direction from God.

Application

When you wake in the morning – what is the first thing you think about? For me, it is a rough outline of what I plan to do that day. The first hour of my day dictates in large part how the rest of the day will go.

If my mind is functioning rightly, I will find time in the first 15 to 30 minutes of each day to sit down with my Bible to read and pray to God. My day has a much better orientation if that time has been properly allocated.

Why – because I have listened to God to get a more clear picture of what I need to do that day. I have set my mind on what is good and truthful.

Yes, there are work, family, personal responsibilities, and chores that I need to accomplish. But I also have people to call or visit that are a part of God's plan for my life. He has a plan for me to bless others and to receive a blessing from others. He has a plan to keep me out of harm's way and to draw me closer to Him.

How in the world am I going to know who I need to reach out to that day if I don't spend time with God and listen to what He has in store for me? He might not change my chores or responsibilities, but He just might have an assignment for me that day that I need to care for.

Bottom line – I need to listen to God early and often each and every day.

Response

How do you spend the first 15 to 30 minutes of each day? Do you spend time listening to God to help you determine what you need to do during the course of that day?

Let God have a say in what you will do today and see how you are able to bless others or how you will be blessed!

Meditation

Read **Proverbs 16:9** in your Bible. Then meditate and journal what God is directing you to do today.

What part of this scripture can you recall all during the day?

Love as Jesus loves

Prayer: God, please forgive me of the things I have done against You, and for the things I should have done for You but didn't. Please speak directly to my heart as I read Your Word. Thank you for how You show me how to love. Please bless our time together.
In the precious name of Jesus I pray,
amen.

This is My command: Love one another as I have loved you. No one has greater love than this, that someone would lay down his life for his friends. You are My friends if you do what I command you.
John 15:12-14

Explanation

In John 15, Jesus is spending time with His closest disciples – those who chose to leave their former life and follow Him. There were others who followed Him, but this was the core group of the twelve disciples.

Jesus was sharing truths with them and speaking in plain talk, not in parables. Jesus spoke the truth in parables so that only those who really wanted to listen and believed that He was the Messiah would understand. This time He was not trying to disguise anything in His dialog to them. Jesus wanted them to understand His direction clearly.

Jesus commanded them to love one another just as He had loved them. The disciples knew just how Jesus had cared for, taught, fed, and loved each one of them. The love He had shown and would show would be the greatest display of love that there ever would be.

It was not a suggestion or advice; it was a solemn command – a directive. Jesus also solidified the command by pointing out that if they considered

Him to be their friend then they would do this very thing – love one another.

He also pointed to the ultimate act of laying down his life to show the greatest way to show love for another. It would be just a few days later that this statement would be completely understood and eternally driven home for each of them.

Application

I think you and I would agree that laying down our life for the love of another is a very tall request. Even sacrificing our life for someone important or dear to us would be utterly difficult. That sacrifice would be so difficult to do, but Jesus explained that very sacrifice for us to use as our ultimate goal.

Our love for Jesus is measured in how we love others. Loving others is the only evidential proof that we indeed love Jesus.

Do you love Jesus? Then you measure how much you love Him by how much you love others.

We can think to ourselves – "Have I loved this or that person enough? Is there any more I could do to love them?" And if the answer to the second question is yes, then there are more ways to love.

The question that comes to my mind is how far should I extend this kind of love? I can think of my wife, kids, or parents, but surely that is far enough. Should I show that same love to my extended family, friends, acquaintances, or even people I don't like?

In the context of what Jesus said, the how far issue was not addressed but implied - everyone. If we model our life after Jesus, then there really is no end to the people we should love. We should strive to love everyone we know this way.

But you and I both know that is difficult. It is hard to love well, even those close to us, but those who are not so close are even harder for us to love.

How on earth will we love one another? By daily focusing on the fact that Jesus told us to do so. Loving others becomes something we get to do because we are friends with Jesus and want to follow His commands.

Now, having that as our mindset doesn't make it much easier, but it does put us in the right mindset to love more because Jesus told me to. Loving others is a lifetime pursuit!

Response

Evaluate how you love those who are close to you.

Evaluate how you love those who are not so close to you.

With the help of Jesus, determine how to love others as Jesus loved His disciples and even you and me today!

Meditation

Read **John 15:9-17** in your Bible. Then meditate and journal what God is saying to you about loving others.

What part of this scripture can you recall all during the day?

The Right Paths

Prayer: God, please forgive me of the things I have done against You, and for the things I should have done for You but didn't. Please speak directly to my heart as I read Your Word. Thank you for having the perfect plans for me. Please bless our time together.
In the precious name of Jesus I pray,
amen.

Trust in the Lord with all your heart, and do not rely on your own understanding; think about Him in all your ways, and He will guide you on the right paths.
Proverbs 3:5-6

Explanation

Solomon tells his son to trust God with everything within himself. He is saying to trust only God, not to put trust in some other person, object, or "little g" god.

Solomon knows there is only one source that can be counted on to be trustworthy – God. He knows from experience that God is dependable, available, and solid.

Our own understanding of situations is limited by the depth and width of the situation as we know it. We know that we have a certain amount of experience, but God knows so much more because He created everything. He knows the past, present, and future. I only know what has happened in the past and the experiences that I have had up to today.

Next Solomon outlines the boundaries for this trust in God - none! In every way that we know and every way we will go, God knows and is already there. That is sort of mind-boggling, but God knows all! Only through our pride do we determine that we know better in a particular situation instead of listening to God.

The result is that God will guide us in the correct ways we should go. God will provide guidance to the right path rather than the wrong path, but one fact remains: we choose which path to take.

Application

Only God is truly trustworthy. The truth of the matter is that I can't always trust even myself to do the right things – even if I know what I should do. I know there are times when I know the right thing to do, but my flesh wins out, and I go down the wrong path. After I get there, sometimes I get so mad at myself for making those decisions.

I find the older I become, the more things I have figured out in this world. But still, my knowledge is only of what I have experienced in life. I only know what I know. There is still so much more that I have not seen or understood, so I need to rely on God to help me choose correctly.

God is the only source I have that will show me the right thing to do in any situation. If I will only slow down and ask, then He will respond. Too often we jump into something without taking the time to ask God which path we should be taking.

This is a daily conversation we should have with God that will help us make wise decisions. Daily, hourly and even moment by moment conversations with God will correctly direct us on the right path.

Response

Take time to ask God for the path you should be taking today. Ask Him which path to take and what you need to be doing on that path.

Stop and ask God again later in the day, and every minute that you possibly can. Never stop asking for His direction.

Then ask the same questions tomorrow, the next day, and the next day, and each and every other tomorrow that you breathe on this earth.

Meditation

Read **Proverbs 3:1-7** in your Bible. Then meditate and journal what God is saying to you.

What part of this scripture can you recall all during the day?

Christian Ethics

Prayer: God, please forgive me of the things I have done against You, and for the things I should have done for You but didn't. Please speak directly to my heart as I read Your Word. Thank you for how You direct me to how I should conduct myself. Please bless our time together. In the precious name of Jesus I pray, amen.

Love must be without hypocrisy. Detest evil; cling to what is good. Show family affection to one another with brotherly love. Outdo one another in showing honor. Do not lack diligence; be fervent in spirit; serve the Lord. Rejoice in hope; be patient in affliction; be persistent in prayer. Share with the saints in their needs; pursue hospitality. Bless those who persecute you; bless and do not curse. Rejoice with those who rejoice; weep with those who weep. Be in agreement with one another. Do not be proud; instead, associate with the humble. Do not be wise in your own estimation. Do not repay anyone evil for evil. Try to do what is honorable in everyone's eyes. If possible, on your part, live at peace with everyone. Friends, do not avenge yourselves; instead, leave room for His wrath. For it is written: Vengeance belongs to Me; I will repay, says the Lord.

Romans 12:9-19

Explanation

Paul outlines to the church in Rome how they should live their daily lives. My Bible has the section heading of "Christian Ethics." Ethics is defined as the rules of conduct, so Christian ethics is basically how a Christian should conduct themselves.

In the first part of Romans 12, Paul is encouraging them to make their bodies a living sacrifice. At this point of his encouragement, he is providing practical details of how to do that. A dead sacrifice cannot come off the altar if it decides not to continue to be a sacrifice, but a living sacrifice does make that choice. Offering our body as a living sacrifice, we daily make the conscious choice to make ourselves presentable to God or not make ourselves presentable.

The list provided is not an exhaustive list of how to be presentable before God, but rather a guideline to which all daily activities could be compared and measured.

Application

In today's world the measure of what is civil and the way we should conduct ourselves is certainly subjective to most. People, organizations, and other beliefs have different ways of defining what moral conduct should look like.

For us as Christians, we have a guide – the Bible. And in the Bible we find all kinds of guidelines, and this one of Paul's is as relevant today as it was when he penned these words to the church in Rome.

Paul doesn't say to not throw your trash out the car window, politely hold the door for others, or make God-pleasing social media posts. We should read these guidelines in their context and compare them to our daily activities as a guide.

I put these in a different format to help us read each individually. Read through these, and if a situation you are in is not covered here, then pray to God and see just what He would say about that situation.

- Love must be without hypocrisy.
- Detest evil; cling to what is good.
- Show family affection to one another with brotherly love.
- Outdo one another in showing honor.
- Do not lack diligence; be fervent in spirit; serve the Lord.
- Rejoice in hope; be patient in affliction.

- Be persistent in prayer.

- Share with the saints in their needs; pursue hospitality.

- Bless those who persecute you; bless and do not curse.

- Rejoice with those who rejoice; weep with those who weep.

- Be in agreement with one another.

- Do not be proud; instead, associate with the humble.

- Do not be wise in your own estimation.

- Do not repay anyone evil for evil.

- Try to do what is honorable in everyone's eyes.

- If possible, on your part, live at peace with everyone.

- Friends, do not avenge yourselves; instead, leave room for His wrath. For it is written: Vengeance belongs to Me; I will repay, says the Lord.

Response

Which of these guidelines do you struggle with? Which are easy for you to follow?

Are there areas in your life that don't fall cleanly into one of these guidelines? Ask God to show you how you should conduct yourself in that situation.

Pray and ask God to show you where you struggle, where He has strengthened you, and how you should respond to either.

Meditation

Read **Romans 12:1-2, 9-21** in your Bible. Then meditate and journal what God is saying to you.

What part of this scripture can you recall all during the day?

Day 18

Discipline of a father

Prayer: God, please forgive me of the things I have done against You, and for the things I should have done for You but didn't. Please speak directly to my heart as I read Your Word. Thank you for allowing me to look at situations differently. Please bless our time together.
In the precious name of Jesus I pray,
amen.

A fool despises his father's discipline, but a person who accepts correction is sensible.
Proverbs 15:5

Explanation

A fool in the Bible is someone who acts unwisely. Solomon says that a fool will disregard or find worthless the discipline of his father. When a father disciplines a child and that child rejects the wisdom provided by the father, the child rejects the father's truth for their own version of truth.

Similarly, Solomon says that the child who accepts the correction from a parental figure is doing the right thing and their mind is making good sense.

Discipline is training someone to follow a prescribed conduct or punishment to correct disobedience. A father has the idea of how his family should behave in private and in public. When a child doesn't follow the behaviors that have been explained, then discipline to that child should happen. That discipline is to change the idea of the child to get in line with the behavior expectations of the family, molding their mind to the direction of the father.

Application

I do not know many people who accept discipline very well – children are a great case in point. Children do not like discipline because it goes against their selfish nature of what they want to do.

Children will test the boundaries of what has been told them, just to see if they can get close and even go over the line that has been drawn.

Adults follow this same line of selfishness as well. One reason for that is that we think that we are always right. For someone else to think differently is upsetting to us. Whether interpreted as an embarrassment or a threat to one's knowledge or skill, no one enjoys being told that they are "wrong." The older we get, the more we think we are always right.

Being disciplined by another person is sometimes embarrassing. Being disciplined by a parent should be correcting. Being disciplined by God should be humbling. In general, discipline should bring about correction.

The fact is that when we are not following the prescribed behaviors of a society, group, family, or workplace, we should be disciplined. The discipline is to bring us back to following the correct behaviors.

Response

In what ways is God disciplining you? In what ways do you reject the discipline that God is providing?

Ask God to show you in your discipline how He wants you to be more like Him and gain wisdom.

Meditation

Read **Proverbs 15:1-7** in your Bible. Then meditate and journal what God is saying to you.

What part of this scripture can you recall all during the day?

Day 19

Fatherly Discipline

Prayer: God, please forgive me of the things I have done against You, and for the things I should have done for You but didn't. Please speak directly to my heart as I read Your Word. Thank you for how You discipline me. Please bless our time together.
In the precious name of Jesus I pray,
amen.

Endure suffering as discipline: God is dealing with you as sons. For what son is there that a father does not discipline? But if you are without discipline — which all receive — then you are illegitimate children and not sons. Furthermore, we had natural fathers discipline us, and we respected them. Shouldn't we submit even more to the Father of spirits and live? For they disciplined us for a short time based on what seemed good to them, but He does it for our benefit, so that we can share His holiness. No discipline seems enjoyable at the time, but painful.
Later on, however, it yields the fruit of peace and righteousness to those who have been trained by it.
Hebrews 12:7-11

Explanation

The writer of Hebrews says that God is dealing with us as His children. Not literally but relating how a good father disciplines his children is similar to the way God disciplines each of us.

He says that if you are not being disciplined by God, then you are not actually one of His children – in other words, not someone who has been saved. The discipline of God is only for those who have repented of their sins and accepted Jesus as their Savior.

Most people will understand that our birth fathers disciplined us, but there are some who never had that privilege. For those who did, we understand that they disciplined us in the way they understood to be good or best for us. Our birth fathers disciplined us according to the rules of their house, the standards they set, and the morals they wanted us to live by.

God disciplines us for our benefit. Our benefit is not only in the short term but for what is best in our life. God also disciplines us to draw us into a closer relationship with Him. God disciplines us according to the rules He wants for His house (our body), the standards He wants us to live our lives by, and the relationship with us that He desires.

Application

I remember when my children were growing up, I had to discipline them. I would try to be consistent in how I disciplined them, but our daughter was over seven years older than our son. And from my experience, girls and boys present different challenges for us parents.

I had the experience of knowing how I disciplined our daughter in my mind as I disciplined our son. I made more mistakes and was probably less consistent with her just because I was learning how to be a father and how to discipline correctly.

I tried to discipline them based on the way my wife and I wanted our children to behave. As parents, we sometimes disagreed on how strictly to enforce those actions. We both had different ideas of discipline based on our own backgrounds and the way our parents disciplined us.

That is a good thing about God. He doesn't have to work out the discipline issue with anyone else. He always knows what is right for our life, and how He wants us to be obedient. He also disciplines in the way that He sees right because He is truth and according to the direction He has planned for our life.

Response

In what ways has God disciplined you in the past that has resulted in peace in your life today? In what ways has God's discipline made you more like Jesus?

Thank God for His discipline in your life - yesterday, today, and tomorrow.

Meditation

Read **Hebrews 12:3-13** in your Bible. Then meditate and journal what God is saying to you about the discipline in your life.

What part of this scripture can you recall all during the day?

Day 20

Seasons of Life

Prayer: God, please forgive me of the things I have done against You, and for the things I should have done for You but didn't. Please speak directly to my heart as I read Your Word. Thank you for having the perfect plans for me during each season of my life.
Please bless our time together.
In the precious name of Jesus I pray,
amen.

There is an occasion for everything, and a time for every activity under heaven: a time to give birth and a time to die;
a time to plant and a time to uproot;
a time to kill and a time to heal;
a time to tear down and a time to build;
a time to weep and a time to laugh;
a time to mourn and a time to dance;
a time to throw stones and a time to gather stones;
a time to embrace and a time to avoid embracing;
a time to search and a time to count as lost;
a time to keep and a time to throw away;
a time to tear and a time to sew;
a time to be silent and a time to speak;
a time to love and a time to hate;
a time for war and a time for peace.
Ecclesiastes 3:1-8

Explanation

Solomon gives a poetic list of the different seasons of life. He not only lists the good things in life, but he also contrasts the darker things of life.

The ebb and flow of the list is not chronological but a recount of events that occur in our life and in all generations. We personally may not experience each, but they are in the world in which we live.

The wisdom shared here from Solomon had come from his years of experience. Solomon recollected these events from his life but also from keen observation of others. He saw and understood that the current season of life that we are experiencing will not remain that way.

Application

The list from Solomon should remind us that we need to take full advantage of the time that God has given us. Each day is a blessing from God, and we should thank Him for what He has in store for us each day.

There will be times of excitement and joy and times of heartache and grief. As humans, we will most likely experience them all at some time in our life.

Embrace the fact that we live through both valley and mountain top experiences. From the valley experiences, we understand to hang on because there is a mountain top to pursue. From the mountain top experience, we should be thankful and know that it will not last forever either.

It is those highs and lows in life that enrich our time here on earth. It is also from our own emotional and physical experiences that we should encourage, mourn, or celebrate with others.

Response

Take time to evaluate your current season of life as you read these words. Thank God for the seasons you have endured, the season in which you live now, and the seasons to come. Be thankful for the good and how you have matured through the bad.

What blessings have you received in this season, and what blessings do you need to share with others?

Meditation

Read **Ecclesiastes 3:1-8** in your Bible. Then meditate and journal what God is saying to you.

What part of this scripture can you recall all during the day?

Day 21

Make Disciples

Prayer: God, please forgive me of the things I have done against You, and for the things I should have done for You but didn't. Please speak directly to my heart as I read Your Word. Thank you for clearly giving the directive to make disciples. Please bless our time together.
In the precious name of Jesus I pray,
amen.

Then Jesus came near and said to them, "All authority has been given to Me in heaven and on earth. Go, therefore, and make disciples of all nations, baptizing them in the name of the Father and of the Son and of the Holy Spirit, teaching them to observe everything I have commanded you. And remember, I am with you always, to the end of the age."

Matthew 28:18-20

Explanation

Jesus had just spent over three years with His disciples, teaching them how to live and share as He wanted. He instructed, demonstrated, and gave them opportunities to practice being disciples of Jesus.

In the ultimate act of humility, they saw him be arrested, beaten, die on a cross, and then resurrect from the dead three days later. After His resurrection, they spent a short amount of time with Him again, confirming His life and deity.

Now he was about to leave them on earth for His heavenly return, and He gave one last directive. Go make disciples.

Go – the go is implied for only those who have repented of their sins and believe that Jesus is their Savior. The Greek meaning of "go" can be thought of as – as you go. He meant as they left that place to where they returned, and as far as they would go on journeys – make disciples of Jesus.

Disciples – the Greek word here is *mathetes* which means an intentional learning of someone or to make a disciple. Disciples in the time of Jesus would study and try to become like a particular scholar. Eventually, the student learned enough to become the next scholar.

All nations – Jesus is directing them to take the Gospel not only to the Jews, but the Gentiles and as far as they knew possible on this earth.

Baptizing – baptizing is the end result of evangelizing with someone and the starting point of their relationship with Jesus, and the beginning of learning how to live a Christian life. It is the outward expression that one has accepted Jesus as their Savior and wants to live like Him.

Teaching them – Jesus instructed His disciples to teach everything that they had learned from Him to those who they baptized.

I am with you – Jesus comforted them by reminding those disciples that He was leaving physically but would remain with them forever spiritually.

Application

My definition of a **disciple** is this:

A student of Jesus who increasingly loves God, increasingly loves others, and helps others do the same.

The Great Commission was not a great suggestion. Just like those disciples that Jesus spoke to that day, we have the directive to make disciples who make disciples of Jesus.

Student - to be a student of Jesus we first must become a believer and follower of Jesus. We must humbly accept and want to follow Jesus. Then we have the pleasure of knowing more about Jeus by studying His life – for the rest of our lives!

Increasingly love God – we are told in Deuteronomy 6:5 to "Love the Lord your God with all your heart, with all your soul, and with all your strength." We do this by spending quality time with God and worshiping Him.

Increasingly love others – if we have the greatest gift of salvation and a relationship with our Creator, why would we not want to share it with others? I show love to others by sharing about the greatest gift I have received, and for those who already follow Jesus, we love them by serving them as needed. As Jesus taught us, we should love one another.

Help others do the same – in Luke 6:40 Jesus said, "a disciple is not above his teacher, but everyone who is fully trained will be like his teacher." We are to spend time with other believers learning to become more like Jesus and to show others how to become more like Jesus!

Response

Are you a disciple of Jesus? If so, how are you increasingly loving God, increasingly loving others, and helping others become disciples?

We all have areas in which we need to develop our spiritual maturity. This is a lifelong journey, not a destination at which you will arrive.

Spend time today and every day becoming more like the disciple of Jesus that He wants you to be.

Meditation

Read **Matthew 28:16-20** in your Bible. Then meditate and journal what God is saying to you.

What part of this scripture can you recall all during the day?

What to do next?

Start your own Bible study using the method we have been following for the past 21 days. Start with John, Matthew, or James. Pick a book in the Bible that you would like to learn more about, and each day use the H.E.A.R. method and the model in this book.

I would like to hear your results by sending a message on my website or social media outlets. You can find them at *blackberrywisdom.com*

Blessed?

Have you been blessed by following this book? I would be honored if you would take just a minute to write an honest review on the *Blackberry Wisdom Bible Study Guide* page of Amazon.

The book will be presented to more people if you will share a short positive review.

Through your Amazon account, you should be able to link directly to this book by searching for *Blackberry Wisdom Bible Study Guide.* I provide a step-by-step guide to the review for those not familiar with Amazon at: *blackberrywisdom.com/guidereview*

Thank you in advance for those who support my ministry and this book!

You just don't know how I have been blessed by writing this book and through the preparation that went into publiging it. I am blessed to be living in this season of my life, and sharing discipleship thoughts with you in this format!

Made in the USA
Columbia, SC
20 May 2023